ENDURING MYSTERIES

BIGFOOT

CHRISTOPHER BAHN

CREATIVE EDUCATION • CREATIVE PAPERBACKS

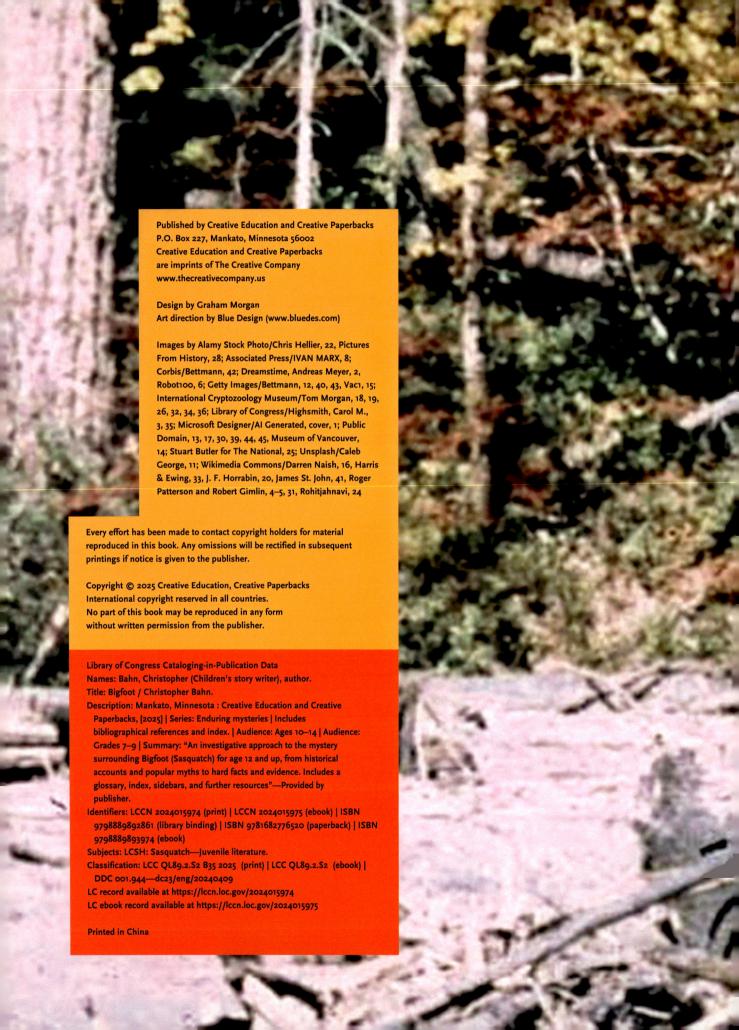

Published by Creative Education and Creative Paperbacks
P.O. Box 227, Mankato, Minnesota 56002
Creative Education and Creative Paperbacks
are imprints of The Creative Company
www.thecreativecompany.us

Design by Graham Morgan
Art direction by Blue Design (www.bluedes.com)

Images by Alamy Stock Photo/Chris Hellier, 22, Pictures From History, 28; Associated Press/IVAN MARX, 8; Corbis/Bettmann, 42; Dreamstime, Andreas Meyer, 2, Robot100, 6; Getty Images/Bettmann, 12, 40, 43, Vac1, 15; International Cryptozoology Museum/Tom Morgan, 18, 19, 26, 32, 34, 36; Library of Congress/Highsmith, Carol M., 3, 35; Microsoft Designer/AI Generated, cover, 1; Public Domain, 13, 17, 30, 39, 44, 45, Museum of Vancouver, 14; Stuart Butler for The National, 25; Unsplash/Caleb George, 11; Wikimedia Commons/Darren Naish, 16, Harris & Ewing, 33, J. F. Horrabin, 20, James St. John, 41, Roger Patterson and Robert Gimlin, 4–5, 31, Rohitjahnavi, 24

Every effort has been made to contact copyright holders for material reproduced in this book. Any omissions will be rectified in subsequent printings if notice is given to the publisher.

Copyright © 2025 Creative Education, Creative Paperbacks
International copyright reserved in all countries.
No part of this book may be reproduced in any form without written permission from the publisher.

Library of Congress Cataloging-in-Publication Data
Names: Bahn, Christopher (Children's story writer), author.
Title: Bigfoot / Christopher Bahn.
Description: Mankato, Minnesota : Creative Education and Creative Paperbacks, [2025] | Series: Enduring mysteries | Includes bibliographical references and index. | Audience: Ages 10–14 | Audience: Grades 7–9 | Summary: "An investigative approach to the mystery surrounding Bigfoot (Sasquatch) for age 12 and up, from historical accounts and popular myths to hard facts and evidence. Includes a glossary, index, sidebars, and further resources"—Provided by publisher.
Identifiers: LCCN 2024015974 (print) | LCCN 2024015975 (ebook) | ISBN 9798889892861 (library binding) | ISBN 9781682776520 (paperback) | ISBN 9798889893974 (ebook)
Subjects: LCSH: Sasquatch—Juvenile literature.
Classification: LCC QL89.2.S2 B35 2025 (print) | LCC QL89.2.S2 (ebook) | DDC 001.944—dc23/eng/20240409
LC record available at https://lccn.loc.gov/2024015974
LC ebook record available at https://lccn.loc.gov/2024015975

Printed in China

Bigfoot, as filmed by Roger Patterson in 1967

CONTENTS

Introduction 9

Bigfoot Country 10

Bigfoot Origins 21

Seeing and Not Believing 29

An Open or Closed Case? 37

Field Notes 46

Selected Bibliography 47

Websites 47

Index 48

INTRODUCTION

OPPOSITE: Pulled from a 16mm film shot by Ivan Marx, this 1977 photo supposedly shows Bigfoot walking in the California wilderness.

In 1967, Roger Patterson was horseback riding through California's Bluff Creek Canyon with a friend, when their horses suddenly reared. Only 60 feet (18 meters) ahead, squatting along the edge of the creek in bright sunlight, was a dark, furry creature. Patterson was certain he'd found what he was looking for: Bigfoot, the **elusive** ape creature of the Pacific Northwest. Patterson had wanted to prove the existence of this legendary beast for many years. He had brought a movie camera with him, but the camera was in a saddlebag, and Patterson had been thrown from his horse. By the time he got the camera and started shooting film, Bigfoot had started moving away.

Patterson filmed Bigfoot walking toward the woods, swinging its long arms with each loping step while looking back at the camera. Patterson filmed the encounter for only about a minute, but that minute has been examined more closely than any Academy Award-winning movie in the past half-century. Was it clear proof, at last, that the giant apelike creature existed? Or, as some said, was the Bigfoot in Patterson's movie just a person in an ape costume? Those answers remain as elusive as Bigfoot itself.

BIGFOOT COUNTRY

OPPOSITE: Densely wooded areas are said to provide prime living conditions for Bigfoot.

I f a creature just wanted to be left alone, some of the wildest and most remote parts of the United States and Canada might be an appealing place to live. Dominated by heavily forested mountains, volcanoes, glaciers, tumbling rivers, and giant redwood trees, the Pacific Northwest offers plenty of hiding spaces. It is home to black bears, cougars, and wolves—animals whose secretiveness, size, and strength have made them some of the most respected and feared creatures on Earth. Some people believe that the area is also home to another large, elusive creature: Bigfoot, also known as Sasquatch.

No one knows for sure if Bigfoot really exists—despite decades of speculation, it is more mystery than fact. People say it is a huge, hairy figure that walks like a human but may be more like a gorilla or a prehistoric form of humanity. It whistles, it smells bad, and it leaves enormous footprints—but little other evidence of its existence. Bigfoot has been the subject of stories of the northwestern woods for centuries.

And creatures like Bigfoot have been figures of legend across North America and the world for just as long. But what is it, exactly? Is it an ape? (If so, it would be the only known ape in the Americas.) Is it some relic of ancient history, such as a **Neanderthal** or other **hominid** that has somehow escaped scientific notice for millions of years? Could it be an ordinary human who has run off to the deep woods because he's embarrassed by his hairy body, bad smell, and monster-sized feet? Could Bigfoot be some kind of extradimensional spirit? Or is it just a bear? Those questions have pestered researchers and travelers in the western woods for generations.

Many people, most scientists included, simply dismiss Bigfoot as a myth. But this is opposed by believers in **cryptozoology**. To them,

OPPOSITE: During a college lecture in 1974, Grover Krantz displayed footprint impressions allegedly made by a Bigfoot.

searching for **cryptids** such as Bigfoot or the Loch Ness Monster and proving their existence is worth any amount of doubt and ridicule.

Although people have been reporting Bigfoot encounters since the 1800s, and similar creatures appear in American Indian folklore from long ago, no one has ever found definitive proof that it exists. People have sometimes claimed to find physical evidence, such as a Bigfoot skull or clumps of hair, but the items have been disproven so far. A study done in 2014 by the University of Oxford found that of 30 samples of hair supposedly taken from Bigfoot or similar cryptids, every one showed molecule traces, or DNA, from common animals such as bears, cows, horses, or humans. Without bones, teeth, or other objects scientists can examine, Bigfoot remains a phantom creature whose existence no one can prove.

CANADIAN POSTAGE STAMP

But what about the tracks? Bigfoot has supposedly left thousands of oversized footprints throughout the woods. Dozens of plaster **casts** of those footprints are stored in colleges, universities, research offices, and the basements of Bigfoot chasers. Using footprints as their starting point, Bigfoot researchers have built a case for the existence of Bigfoot, literally from the ground up.

The name "Bigfoot" usually means just the creature that lives in the Pacific Northwest. Grover Krantz (1931–2002), an **anthropologist** at Washington State University and one of the few scholars to give Bigfoot stories serious consideration, estimated there could be 2,000

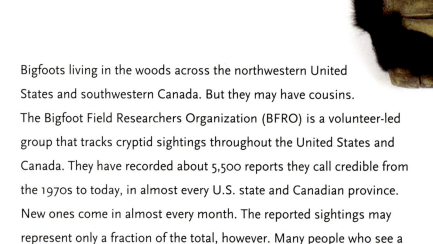

RIGHT: A Sasq'ets (Sasquatch) mask carved by the Sts'ailes people of British Columbia, Canada

Bigfoots living in the woods across the northwestern United States and southwestern Canada. But they may have cousins. The Bigfoot Field Researchers Organization (BFRO) is a volunteer-led group that tracks cryptid sightings throughout the United States and Canada. They have recorded about 5,500 reports they call credible from the 1970s to today, in almost every U.S. state and Canadian province. New ones come in almost every month. The reported sightings may represent only a fraction of the total, however. Many people who see a Bigfoot keep the story to themselves, out of fear of ridicule.

Sightings of similar Bigfoot-type cryptids across the United States include the Skunk Ape in Florida and the Fouke Monster of Arkansas. In other countries around the world—on every continent except Antarctica—they've been given names such as *yeti*, *yowie*, *almas*, *yeren*, and *orang pendek*. If these creatures indeed exist, we don't know whether they're the same animal as Bigfoot or a related species. The majority of sightings have been in the Pacific Northwest, where forest-dwelling American Indians have long told stories of these huge, apelike beings. The Halkomelem people called the beings Sasq'ets. In 1929, a Canadian journalist named J. W. Burns collected some of their stories for the magazine *Maclean's* and wrote the name as "Sasquatch," which he said meant "the hairy mountain men." This is the name for Bigfoot most often used in Canada.

In 1958, workers building a road in the woods overlooking Bluff Creek in northern California were astonished to find huge footprints around their construction equipment. One of the workers, Jerry Crew,

YETI

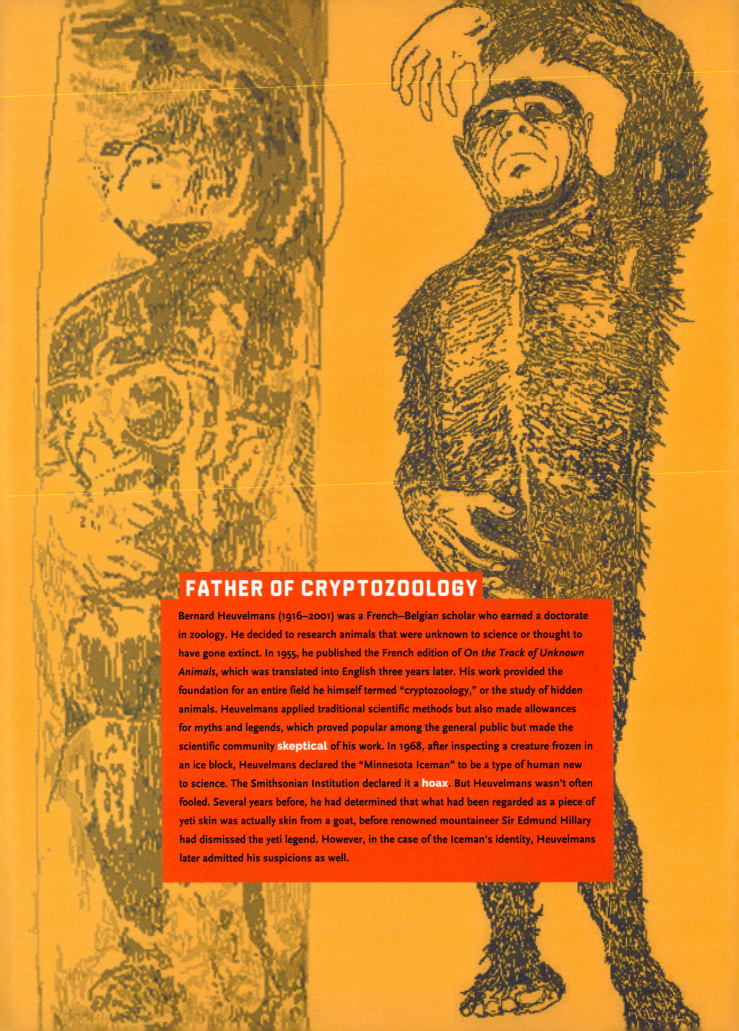

FATHER OF CRYPTOZOOLOGY

Bernard Heuvelmans (1916–2001) was a French–Belgian scholar who earned a doctorate in zoology. He decided to research animals that were unknown to science or thought to have gone extinct. In 1955, he published the French edition of *On the Track of Unknown Animals*, which was translated into English three years later. His work provided the foundation for an entire field he himself termed "cryptozoology," or the study of hidden animals. Heuvelmans applied traditional scientific methods but also made allowances for myths and legends, which proved popular among the general public but made the scientific community **skeptical** of his work. In 1968, after inspecting a creature frozen in an ice block, Heuvelmans declared the "Minnesota Iceman" to be a type of human new to science. The Smithsonian Institution declared it a **hoax**. But Heuvelmans wasn't often fooled. Several years before, he had determined that what had been regarded as a piece of yeti skin was actually skin from a goat, before renowned mountaineer Sir Edmund Hillary had dismissed the yeti legend. However, in the case of the Iceman's identity, Heuvelmans later admitted his suspicions as well.

made plaster casts of some of the prints near his job site. Pictures of the 16-inch-long (41-centimeter) footprints showed up within days on the front page of California's *Humboldt Times*, and the name "Bigfoot," coined by *Times* columnist Andrew Genzoli, exploded into the vocabulary of everyday Americans.

Descriptions of the creature known as Bigfoot or Sasquatch are remarkably consistent: an upright woodland creature that has 5-toed, flat feet measuring up to 27 inches (69 cm) long and 7 to 12 inches (18–31 cm) wide. Bigfoot's big toe lines up with its other four toes, unlike an ape's, which points off like a thumb so it can be used for grasping. The prints attributed to Bigfoot don't show claws, as a bear's would. Prints found to be several inches deep in the forest floor have meant that the creature that made them could weigh from several hundred to 1,000 pounds (454 kilograms). Such are the outlines the footprints have provided. People claiming to have encountered Bigfoot and even photographed it have filled in the rest of the details.

THE ORIGINS OF CRYPTOZOOLOGY

BIGFOOT COUNTRY

The creature could be 7 to 8 feet (2.1–2.4 m) tall and covered on all but its face, palms, and feet with black, brown, reddish, or white hair. It is said that Bigfoot can scream, grunt, moan, or whoop, but it most often makes a whistling sound. Its smell is distinctively awful—like rotten eggs or a dead animal. This is one reason why, in Florida, it is called the Skunk Ape. The creature is fast on its feet, too, having been clocked running

17

alongside vehicles at 45 to 70 miles (72–113 kilometers) per hour. Its most bizarre features, though, may be eyes that seem to glow red, pink, green, or white in the dark, not just as reflections but at times with what appears to be their own bright light.

Bigfoot apparently eats just about anything: roots, berries, nuts, pine needles, and even rodents, rabbits, clams, or chickens. But where does Bigfoot sleep? How big are its babies? Can it climb trees? How long does it live? Can one Bigfoot communicate with another? Do they form communities? Do their habits change in the winter? If they resemble humans so much, why don't they seek out contact with people? No one knows.

In today's world, Bigfoot may no longer be able to avoid people. With the human population expanding, and with people finding more ways to explore and work in remote areas, Bigfoot's secret lair could be shrinking. New technology such as night-vision scopes, heat sensors, satellite-based tracking, and high-powered telescopes and sound equipment could expose Bigfoot more readily in its home. The BFRO monitors and evaluates sightings, collects information and identifies hoaxes, and organizes expeditions to find Bigfoot while maintaining a policy that it will study Bigfoot only in ways that do the creature no harm.

But the scientific community and the media alike would be shocked and thrilled if anyone ever found a Bigfoot bone, not to mention an entire skeleton or skin. It would rewrite what's known of the history of human evolution. And for those in the movie business, there's no telling how much money could be made from showing the world a real live Bigfoot.

Would proof of Bigfoot's existence and a detailed understanding of the creature add to or detract from its well-known reputation? Maybe neither. But a little mystery—or a lot of it—is also important, some insist. "We need to experience awe," wrote the former director of the Smithsonian Institution's Primate Biology Program, John Napier, in 1973. "Man needs his gods—and his monsters—and the more remote and unapproachable they are, the better."

1975 NEWSPAPER CLIPPING

Elusive Bigfoot Gets Official Recognition by U.S. Army

The U.S. Army has officially recognized Bigfoot, the legendary "ape-like creature" that stalks the wilds of the Pacific Northwest and Russia.

The recognition — first ever by a U.S. government agency — came in the latest environmental atlas published by the Army Corps of Engineers, which devotes an entire page to the mysterious creature.

Bigfoot was included in "The Washington Environmental Atlas" because "there is so much overwhelming evidence that points to such a creature," explained Jean McManus, who is editor of the reference work.

"The details about the creature were gathered from many sources — anthropologists, writers and genuine Bigfoot hunters. A great deal of time and effort has gone into hunting this creature, and it seemed only right to include it in the book."

The atlas also reveals that the FBI conducted extensive laboratory tests on hair believed to have come from Bigfoot.

The FBI concluded that "the hair was not from any human or from any known animal form," the official Army volume said. FBI headquarters in the nation's capital and its offices in Oregon and Washington were unable to provide any details of the reported lab analyses.

The atlas describes Bigfoot, based on alleged sightings, this way:

"An ape-like creature, 8 to 12 feet in height, weighing around 1,000 pounds, covered in long hair apart from the face and palms of the hands and feet.

"The footprints are up to 24 inches in length and 5 to 10 inches wide. Bigfoot is very agile and powerful."

Maj. Fred Shierley, an Army spokesman at the Pentagon, said: "This is the first time there has ever been official Army reference to the actual existence of Bigfoot. As far as we know, no other government agency has recognized its possible existence before.

"We believe the Army is the first agency to do it."

The Army's action was "encouraging" news to Dr. Geoffrey Bourne, director of the prestigious Yerkes Regional Primate Research Center of Emory University in Atlanta.

"I believe that Bigfoot could be a Giganto Pithecus that was known to exist about 750,000 years ago and looks like a part ape, part man," he told The ENQUIRER.

Bigfoot has been sighted hundreds of times, according to Prof. Grover Krantz, a University of Washington anthropologist, and Ron Olson, executive director of the North American Wildlife Research Assn., who have studied casts of the animal's massive footprints.

Prof. Krantz said he hoped the Army would now lend its support to an all-out effort to capture one of the creatures for scientific study.

Olson said his organization has fed reported sightings of the creature into a computer to trace a pattern of its movements.

"With some help, and a bit of luck, I feel we could catch Bigfoot in two years," he declared.

— ARTHUR GOLDEN

BIGFOOT as an artist's sketch shows him in new reference atlas.

BIGFOOT ORIGINS

OPPOSITE: Neanderthals were cousins of modern humans who lived in Europe and southwestern and central Asia.

Scientists may or may not believe in Bigfoot, but they do agree that it wasn't all that long ago that humans shared the world with other almost-people—**bipedal** hominids related to humans, but not the same as modern *homo sapiens*. Humans and other hominids, presumably including Bigfoot, evolved from an apelike common ancestor perhaps 5 to 10 million years ago. Being bipedal freed their hands for hunting, gathering, and carrying things. These creatures could live more advanced lives than their primate relatives, the apes. Their diet improved, and their brains grew because of it. Tools, fire, and speech followed. **Fossil** evidence shows that some human cousins, such as the Neanderthals and Denisovans, lived right alongside humans before dying out 30,000 to 50,000 years ago. In one sense, they did not die out at all, since their DNA is found in some modern humans, which makes them the direct ancestors of some people living today. But to the

OPPOSITE: An illustration from the early 1900s depicts Bigfoot as an apelike bipedal creature.

best understanding of scientists, humans have been the only hominids left on Earth for at least 30,000 years.

If Bigfoot somehow survived as a species alongside humans, how could it survive, while the others didn't? And how could it leave no fossils behind, when the others did? Why hasn't there been more evidence in the form of dens or cave sites, teeth, or bones? Bigfoot evidently never mastered fire, writing, tool development, or cooking. Why not, if it supposedly has so many other human qualities? And even so, shouldn't it have left traces of a meal somewhere over the ages? Perhaps most importantly, if it lives in North America, where humans have lived for only 13,000 years, when and how did it get here? If Bigfoot is as much ape as human, what's it doing in the Pacific Northwest, where the weather can be far colder than it is in the tropics, where most apes thrive? As long as no one is sure what Bigfoot *is*, it will be difficult to answer all of those questions.

Anthropologists have long believed that humans originated in Africa and then spread across Europe and Asia, reaching Australia by sea around 50,000 years ago. Humans got to North America, home of Bigfoot, much more recently—about 13,000 years ago, when the last glaciers retreated and exposed a land bridge that connected the eastern tip of present-day Russia to what is now Alaska, across the Bering Sea. (Some recent findings suggest humans may have reached the continent at least 10,000 years earlier.) Cryptozoologists say Bigfoot probably came to North America the same way. And those same researchers say that

OPPOSITE: Hairy yetis depicted in Himalayan artwork may be based on a rare species of brown bear.

long before that, Bigfoot might have descended from a relative that they know actually existed in Asia: *Gigantopithecus*.

In 1935, German scientist Ralph von Koenigswald (1902–82) was rummaging through Chinese medicine shops and bought some "dragon's teeth"—fossils the Chinese people would grind into powder to make medicines. In fact, he was looking for the teeth of extinct mammals. In a Hong Kong shop, von Koenigswald found the tooth of an apelike animal that would had to have been twice the size of a gorilla. Then in 1950, Italian scientists in China found a fossilized jawbone they traced to this huge, extinct ape as well. Only jawbones and teeth of this animal have ever been found, but those were enough to determine that it was the largest primate ever to walk the earth. The most recent science says that *Gigantopithecus* lived between 2 million and 300,000 years ago. It was nearly 10 feet (3 m) tall and weighed up to 650 pounds (295 kg), making it far larger than the largest known ape, the 500-pound (227-kg) silverback male gorilla. It lived in northern India, China, and southeast Asia, and it is believed to have been a "knuckle-walker," like an ape. Scientists believe it may have gone extinct because humans and giant pandas may have eaten too much of its primary food: bamboo. Or—maybe—it could have wandered off and become Bigfoot.

Bigfoot is just one of many secretive "ape men" cryptids to have been sighted in remote areas around the world. Its most famous cousin is probably the yeti, thought to roam the rugged, tall peaks of Asia's Himalayan Mountains. The yeti is also known as the "Abominable Snowman," although the Chinese word

NEANDERTHAL SKULL

more accurately means "wild man of the snows." The yeti appears in Himalayan religious art, and monks keep what they say are yeti skins in their mountain retreats. Reports of yeti sightings are common among Sherpas, people who live in Nepal and frequently serve as guides on mountain-climbing expeditions. The first report of a yeti sighting from a European was in 1889, when British explorer Major L. A. Waddell thought he spotted one in the Himalayas.

The yeti is said to be a shaggy, stooped creature that lives in caves at altitudes of 12,000 to 20,000 feet (3,658–6,096 m). But, as with Bigfoot, most of the evidence is based on footprints, and a yeti's prints are not much larger than a person's. In 1951, mountaineer Eric Shipton photographed what he said was a line of prints a mile (1.6 km) long in the mountain snows. It looked **authentic**, but scientists discounted it, saying it could have been another animal's footprint that expanded as the snow melted in the sun. In 1960, Sir Edmund Hillary (who, along

BIGFOOT THE ALIEN?

Skeptics often say the lack of definitive Bigfoot evidence simply means the creature doesn't exist. But some Bigfoot believers have a surprising answer to that: Bigfoot has supernatural powers and may not be from Earth. Jack Lapseritis, author of *The Psychic Sasquatch*, claims that Bigfoot and his kind are actually gentle, advanced forms of humans who speak to him **telepathically** and have been visiting Earth for millions of years. Other cryptozoologists report that people have seen Bigfoot holding a mysterious glowing orange orb, leading to speculation that the creature uses magical portals to vanish into a dimension beyond Earth. Lapseritis offers some dos and don'ts for contacting a Sasquatch:

DON'T: Stalk it with weapons or cameras (or with a desire to make money off the encounter). Aggressiveness will keep it away.

DO: Meditate, envision a Sasquatch, and invite it to visit. Then do something else. The Sasquatch will appear when it chooses to.

with Sherpa Tenzing Norgay, was the first to summit Mount Everest in 1953) returned to the area in part to look for yeti. He found nothing and echoed earlier suggestions that yeti prints were those of other animals. He also famously said that the skins that Himalayan monks collected were not from yeti but from a goat known as a serow, and that many yeti stories and sightings might have originated with Sherpas who had embellished the tales. Some researchers have asserted that solitary footprints in snow at high altitudes in the Himalayas may have actually been made by monks walking from one valley to another. In 1995, the Chinese Academy of Sciences issued a report stating that 95 percent of yeti sightings are false and the creature does not exist. But sightings continue to be reported.

Australia also has its share of sightings of a large, reclusive, hairy figure. The yowie is reportedly 7 to 12 feet (2.1 to 3.7 m) tall, with long arms and humanlike hands. Like Bigfoot, it's been described as having a repulsive body odor akin to rotting garbage or vomit. It also has glowing eyes like Bigfoot. But it is more adapted to its human neighbors, with sightings most commonly reported along the populated eastern side of the continent. In fact, the creature is often reported peering in windows or following people in the woods. Like Bigfoot, footprints are its only traces, but these vary in size and in form. Some are three-toed, and some are five-toed.

SEEING AND NOT BELIEVING

OPPOSITE: In Himalayan folklore, yetis ranged in color from nearly black to pure white.

Undoubtedly, most people have been introduced to Bigfoot by Roger Patterson's famous fuzzy short film from 1967, showing a broad-backed, long-armed, thick-shouldered biped with a whitish face, a purposeful stride, and a thick coat of dark hair. Patterson was a former rodeo rider with such a deep interest in Bigfoot that he wrote a book in 1966 called *Do Abominable Snowmen of America Really Exist?* He was also a wildlife photographer who was working on his own **documentary** film. In October 1967, he and his friend Bob Gimlin went out looking for a Bigfoot in an area near Willow Creek, California, where there had been many sightings over the years. And there it was. Patterson's film is the only "clear" photographic image of a Bigfoot ever recorded. Patterson died only five years after making it, insisting until the end that it was genuine. Gimlin also stands by the story. Krantz, the Washington State University anthropologist, has said he believes the film to be authentic,

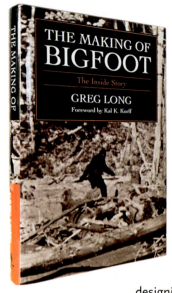

OPPOSITE: Despite many theories, no one has been able to prove that Patterson's Bigfoot wasn't real.

too. Others say the creature's apparently muscular legs and arms are convincing.

But the Patterson film has far more detractors than supporters. Naysayers claim that the size and motion of the figure in the film make clear that it is a human in a padded ape suit. For years, it was widely believed that Hollywood makeup artist John Chambers, who won an Academy Award for designing the masks in the 1968 film *Planet of the Apes*, had designed Patterson's ape suit. Chambers denied it, reportedly saying he was "good but . . . not that good." Another costume-maker, Philip Morris, told Greg Long, author of *The Making of Bigfoot: The Inside Story*, that he made the costume and sold it to Patterson, with advice on how to pad the shoulders, extend the arms, and make the head bigger by wearing a football helmet underneath. Long also interviewed a friend of Patterson's, Bob Heironimus, who well after Patterson's death claimed that he had worn the suit and played Bigfoot in Patterson's film. The suit has never been found.

Although the Patterson film is the most famous Bigfoot sighting, there have been hundreds of other tales through the years. More recent reports describe only fleeting glimpses or footprints, suggesting an apparently shy creature. But the older stories of Bigfoot encounters often portray the creature as an aggressive monster. In 1893, future U.S. president Theodore Roosevelt wrote of a shocking encounter in his book *The Wilderness Hunter*. Roosevelt told of meeting a "grizzled, weather-beaten old mountain hunter" named Bauman who "knew well the stories of the snow-walkers and the spectres and the formless evil beings that haunt the forest depths." Bauman told Roosevelt that years

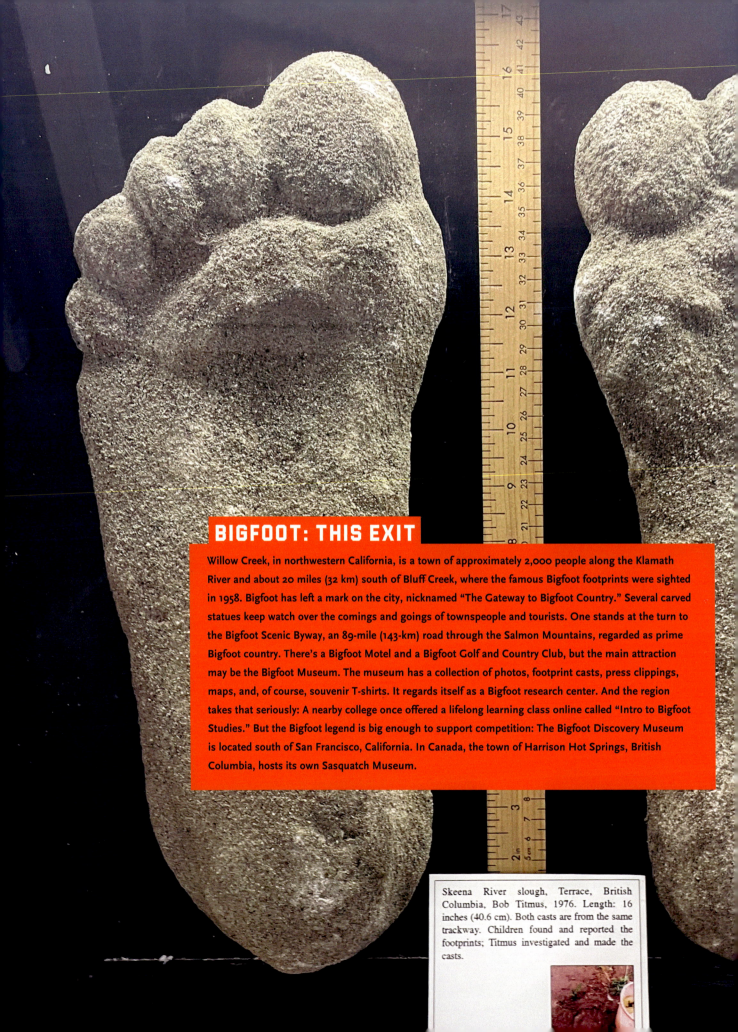

BIGFOOT: THIS EXIT

Willow Creek, in northwestern California, is a town of approximately 2,000 people along the Klamath River and about 20 miles (32 km) south of Bluff Creek, where the famous Bigfoot footprints were sighted in 1958. Bigfoot has left a mark on the city, nicknamed "The Gateway to Bigfoot Country." Several carved statues keep watch over the comings and goings of townspeople and tourists. One stands at the turn to the Bigfoot Scenic Byway, an 89-mile (143-km) road through the Salmon Mountains, regarded as prime Bigfoot country. There's a Bigfoot Motel and a Bigfoot Golf and Country Club, but the main attraction may be the Bigfoot Museum. The museum has a collection of photos, footprint casts, press clippings, maps, and, of course, souvenir T-shirts. It regards itself as a Bigfoot research center. And the region takes that seriously: A nearby college once offered a lifelong learning class online called "Intro to Bigfoot Studies." But the Bigfoot legend is big enough to support competition: The Bigfoot Discovery Museum is located south of San Francisco, California. In Canada, the town of Harrison Hot Springs, British Columbia, hosts its own Sasquatch Museum.

Skeena River slough, Terrace, British Columbia, Bob Titmus, 1976. Length: 16 inches (40.6 cm). Both casts are from the same trackway. Children found and reported the footprints; Titmus investigated and made the casts.

THEODORE ROOSEVELT

before, he and his partner were stalked in the woods by a smelly, two-legged creature. Each day, when they returned from checking and setting traps, they would find their camp destroyed. One night, Bauman heard a commotion outside his tent and fired his shotgun toward the noise. Whatever it was ran off. The next day, when Bauman came back from checking traps, he found his partner dead with a broken neck.

Another story involved five miners in a cabin on Washington's Mount St. Helens in 1924. One day one of the miners saw a Bigfoot and fired at it. That night, their cabin was attacked by several Bigfoots, one of which even punched through the wall. The attack lasted five hours. Although that story, too, was later dismissed, it caused enough excitement at the time that the area was named Ape Canyon.

That same year, a logger named Albert Ostman, who was searching for gold in British Columbia, was carried and dragged for three hours in his sleeping bag, unable to reach his knife to cut himself free. At dawn he found himself in a camp with a family of Bigfoots—what appeared to be a father, a mother, a young male, and a young female. Ostman was closely watched for six days until he offered the 8-foot-tall (2.4-m) adult male Bigfoot his tin of tobacco. The Bigfoot ate it and, either sick or disgusted, ran off to a creek for a drink. That's when Ostman escaped, firing a shot back at the adult female. Ostman didn't tell his story for 33 years—he said he thought no one would believe him. Some say that because he waited until other stories started emerging, his story isn't credible. Others say that the fact he recalled so much detail, including how he was first lifted at 4:25 A.M. (he had been able to look at his

SEEING AND NOT BELIEVING

33

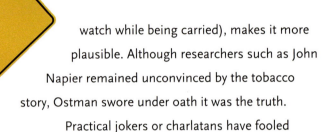

watch while being carried), makes it more plausible. Although researchers such as John Napier remained unconvinced by the tobacco story, Ostman swore under oath it was the truth.

Practical jokers or charlatans have fooled people with made-up Bigfoot evidence for many years. Some—though not all—of the more famous Bigfoot encounters have been later been discredited by admitted hoaxers who just wanted to have some fun or rustle up some tourist dollars. The family of Ray Wallace, the foreman on the 1958 Bluff Creek road crew that found footprints that led to the name "Bigfoot," said after Wallace died that he had made the prints from wooden blocks. Another man named Rant Mullens has said that he and his uncle were behind the 1924 Ape Canyon incident, throwing rocks in the dark to scare the miners and later manufacturing his own set of fake feet to make tracks with. In 1969, some huge footprints found near Bossburg, Washington, attracted a spotlight, even though they were "found" by an amateur naturalist with a reputation as a practical joker. However, the Smithsonian's Napier and anthropologist Krantz both said it was unlikely that a footprint like that could have been faked. "It is very difficult to conceive of a hoaxer so subtle, so knowledgeable—and so sick—who would deliberately fake a footprint of this nature," Napier wrote. "I suppose it is possible, but it is so unlikely that I am prepared to discount it."

Darren Naish, a British **paleontologist** and the author of *Hunting Monsters: Cryptozoology and the Reality Behind the Myths*, disagrees, saying that a major problem for Bigfoot is a "persisting lack of good evidence: what's been presented so far, what exists so far, still doesn't cut it." But believers argue that the sheer number of reported sightings means that

Harriett McFeely, the self-proclaimed "Bigfoot Lady of Hastings, Nebraska," opened her Bigfoot museum in 2018.

they can't all be fake. Bigfoot sightings have continued, despite naysayers and doubts. The BFRO has logged new reports of Bigfoot sightings that it regards as credible on its website since 1995. Many of those sightings were from years ago and based on memory, but the BFRO promises that its researchers personally investigate each claim to determine credibility.

AN OPEN OR CLOSED CASE?

OPPOSITE: One thing every Bigfoot has is plenty of hair!

Bigfoot's run-ins with humans, while often startling, have been few and far between. Yet reports of similar hairy cryptids have been made all across North America. These creatures have usually been sighted in rural areas. And they don't always match all the classic Bigfoot characteristics. Most have been tall, but some have been short. Some had glowing eyes. Some, three toes. Some, three legs. In some cases, gunshots have seemed to go right through them.

After Roosevelt's report in 1893, other sightings became known. According to a woman who wrote to researcher Ivan Sanderson, two hunters in northern Minnesota in 1911 saw a gigantic, hairy human with long arms that left strange footprints. In Effingham, Illinois, a woman named Beulah Schroat said her brothers had often seen hairy creatures near their home. In 1941, the Reverend Lepton Harpole, hunting squirrels along a

OPPOSITE: A 1965 newspaper article details an encounter with the "Monroe Monster."

creek in Mt. Vernon, Illinois, reported that a large creature that "looked something like a baboon" jumped out of a tree. The beast followed him on two feet, until the reverend whacked it with his gun barrel and fired some shots into the air, causing it to flee. Hunters and rural residents in the area over the next few months heard frightening screaming sounds and found strange footprints. Some said the creature could jump 20 to 40 feet (6.1–12 m) in the air.

Many would say that modern America is more skeptical and less superstitious than it was in those days. Nevertheless, reports of cryptid encounters have become more common.

AMONG THE STORIES:

- Christine Van Acker, a 17-year-old girl from Monroe, Michigan, got a black eye on August 11, 1965, after a 7-foot-tall (2.1-m) hairy giant stepped into the road in front of the car her mother was driving, approached the car, reached in, and grabbed the girl. The girl screamed, and nearby workers responded as the creature retreated. It was later known as the "Monroe Monster."
- In 1969, George Kaiser, a farmer near Rising Sun, Indiana, watched a 5-foot-8 (1.7-m) hairy creature with humanlike hands for about 2 minutes at a distance of about 25 feet (7.6 m) before it ran off, leaving large, 4-toed prints behind.
- In 1975, Noxie, Oklahoma, farmer Kenneth Tosh and his neighbors reported seeing a pair of hairy creatures that stood more than 6 feet (1.8 m) tall. The screaming beasts had glowing eyes and smelled like rotten eggs.
- In 1990, Helen Smythe Wilson of Roachdale, Indiana, told an interviewer that "sometime ago" there had been many reports in

PEOPLE IN THE NEWS
Manry Tells of Hallucinations at Sea

Compiled From The Independent's Wire Services

Robert Manry, a lone newsman-mariner from Ohio, went ashore at Falmouth, England, Tuesday night after a 78-day voyage from Cape Cod, Mass., in a 13½-foot sailboat — the smallest known to have made the eastward Atlantic crossing nonstop.

Hailed as a hero, the 47-year-old Manry, of Cleveland, first embraced his wife and two children and knelt to kiss the soil of England. Then at a news conference he told a spine-chilling story of fear, exhaustion and hallucinations at sea.

Six times he was washed overboard from the tiny Tinkerbelle and saved by a lifeline.

Amid a storm of cheers, Manry stepped from the Tinkerbelle onto the Custom House Quay. He had been at sea 2½ months on the 3,200-mile crossing.

Both man and boat looked immaculate. Tinkerbelle proudly flew the Stars and Stripes.

At his news conference with his wife beside him, Manry told a nightmare story of hallucinations and exhaustion.

Exhaustion, he explained, was his greatest fear. To fight it, he took a medicine, and it had spine-chilling effects, he said.

"For a time I thought my boy Douglas was on the boat with me," he said.

"Then there was another man with us — a monster — and when Douglas went into the cabin, this monster would throw him overboard. I got so I was scared to go into the cabin for fear of this monster.

"Eventually, I plucked up the courage to jump in there. There was no one there, and that broke the hallucination."

Another time, he said, he had the impression of sailing on a huge sea mountain.

"I was looking for something — and wasted a whole day just milling about until I snapped out of it," he stated.

He figured on 60 to 75 days for the trip. It took 78.

REJECTED
A Soviet appeal court Tuesday rejected an appeal by British teacher Gerald Brooke against a five-year sentence on charges of subversive anti-Soviet activities.

The collegium, or main panel, of the supreme court of the Russian Federation for Criminal Affairs confirmed the sentence given Brooke July 23 by a Moscow city court.

Brooke was sentenced to one year in prison and four years at hard labor for attempts to conduct subversive activities in Moscow in behalf of a Russian emigre organization.

NO ALARM
Vatican sources Tuesday said they saw no cause for alarm over Pope Paul VI's health despite reports that he may have a small ulcer which is slowing his recovery from overexertion.

The report was published in an article in the weekly magazine Tempo. A high Vatican source Monday said "there may well be a slight ulcerous condition but I am not at all preoccupied that the Pope's health is gravely threatened."

No official denial or confirmation of the report was forthcoming from the Vatican thus far.

CONFIRM
The Senate Foreign Relations Committee Tuesday approved President Johnson's nomination of Robert Wood Akers to be deputy director of the U.S. Information Agency (USIA).

NOVELIST DIES
Jun Takami, 58, one of Japan's foremost novelists, died of cancer of the esophagus Tuesday in Tokyo.

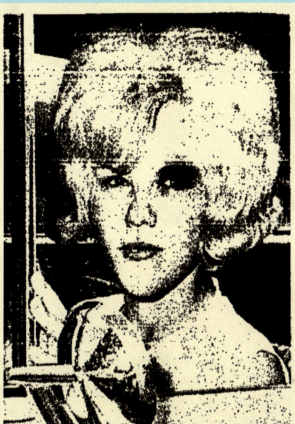

—AP Wirephoto
CHRISTINE VAN ACKER ... Black Eye From "Monster"

SEARCH FOR THE 'MONSTER'
A throng of curious estimated by police to have numbered 1,000 went monster hunting Monday night in weather which on sheriff's deputy said "no monster in his right mind would be out in."

They congregated, at times creating monumental, bumper-to-bumper traffic jams, a few miles north of Monroe, Mich., in Frenchtown township. It is there in Michigan's southeastern corner that monster reports have developed off and on since June.

As far as deputies and state police were concerned there were no "confirmed" sightings during the night.

"We're not treating it completely as a hoax," Cpl. David Swanson of the Flat Rock post said. "We're still investigating."

At least 15 persons claim to have seen the monster. Mrs. George Ownes, 38, says she and her daughter, Christine Van Acker, 17, of Monroe, were attacked in their car by something last Friday.

They described it as a black, 7-foot, 400-pound, grunting "thing" covered with hair.

"He reached through the window and grabbed my hair," said Christine. She demonstrated a black eye where she said it slugged her.

"He was all hairy," Christine said, "and the hairs were like quills. They pricked whenever I touched them."

SLOW PROGRESS
Former Sen. Barry Goldwater is making slow but steady progress in his re-

NO ASTERISK
Morey McDaniel lost his fight Tuesday in San Francisco to have an asterisk

Phil Thompson poses with an alleged Bigfoot footprint in Oregon in 1976.

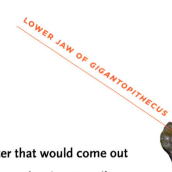

LOWER JAW OF GIGANTOPITHECUS

her town of a hairy monster that would come out at night to raid chicken coops, leaving "a trail of feathers and blood" in its wake. The monster eventually disappeared.

- Between 1977 and 1993, people in Tuscola County, Michigan, reported encounters with cryptids on farms and roads 38 different times. That's more than two sightings per year. A video showing a creature crossing a local river went viral on the Internet in 2021.
- Today, both news media and the BFRO tell stories of campers, drivers, forest workers, and others—some searching for Bigfoot, others caught completely by surprise—who report piercing sounds at night; sightings of big, hairy, two-legged creatures crossing roads; and face-to-face encounters.

Pursuing mysteries is fundamental to science. But to find answers, scientists need evidence that can be examined—something they can measure or put under a microscope. Even though no human has ever seen a living *Tyrannosaurus rex*, much is known about it because the animal left behind so many bones, which tell scientists how the dinosaur lived. But Bigfoot is another matter. Somehow, a creature that some believe has lived alongside humans for tens of thousands of years hasn't left a single bone behind. It's not unheard of—*Gigantopithecus* is known only

AN OPEN OR CLOSED CASE?

41

DR. JANE GOODALL

from teeth and a few partial jawbones. But it's also unlikely, and that's one reason why many scientists don't take Bigfoot stories seriously.

Grover Krantz and Dr. Jeff Meldrum, associate professor of anatomy and anthropology at Idaho State University, think Bigfoot deserves sober consideration. Meldrum says he paid little attention to Bigfoot until he came across fresh tracks in 1996. He thinks scientists aren't giving enough weight to eyewitness accounts of Bigfoot. And that, he writes in his book *Sasquatch: Legend Meets Science*, means they might be missing a good story. Finding and documenting Bigfoot, he writes, "may eventually prove to be among the most astounding zoological discoveries ever."

Dr. Jane Goodall, a primate scientist who is regarded as the world's expert on chimpanzees, says she was told by villagers in Ecuador of 6-foot-tall (1.8-m) apelike creatures that walk upright. She notes that the worldwide spread of stories about Bigfoot-like creatures suggests that the mythology has been part of humanity for a long time and might echo long-forgotten encounters with Neanderthals. She told the magazine *GQ* in 2021 that she was keeping an open mind: "I don't know. But I'm not going to say it doesn't exist, and I'm not going to say people who believe in it are stupid."

DON'T SHOOT!

In 1969, Skamania County (Washington) commissioners passed a law making it illegal to kill a Bigfoot. They acknowledged that both legend and "recent sightings and **spoor**" supported the possibility that Bigfoot was roaming in southwestern Washington. They added that publicity about Bigfoot had drawn so many people with guns into the woods that a ban was needed to protect "the safety and well-being of persons living or traveling within the boundaries of Skamania County as well as . . . the creatures themselves." The ordinance was passed on April 1, making some people think it was a joke. But it was later amended to make shooting a Bigfoot a crime akin to murder—which also made Bigfoot the legal equivalent of a human being. In the state's northwestern corner, Whatcom County, along the Canadian border north of Seattle, declared itself in 1992 to be a "Sasquatch Protection and Refuge Area." However, hunting officials in states such as Texas have said that as long as Bigfoot is not known to science, not classified as being endangered, and not mentioned in hunting laws, people can hunt it any time.

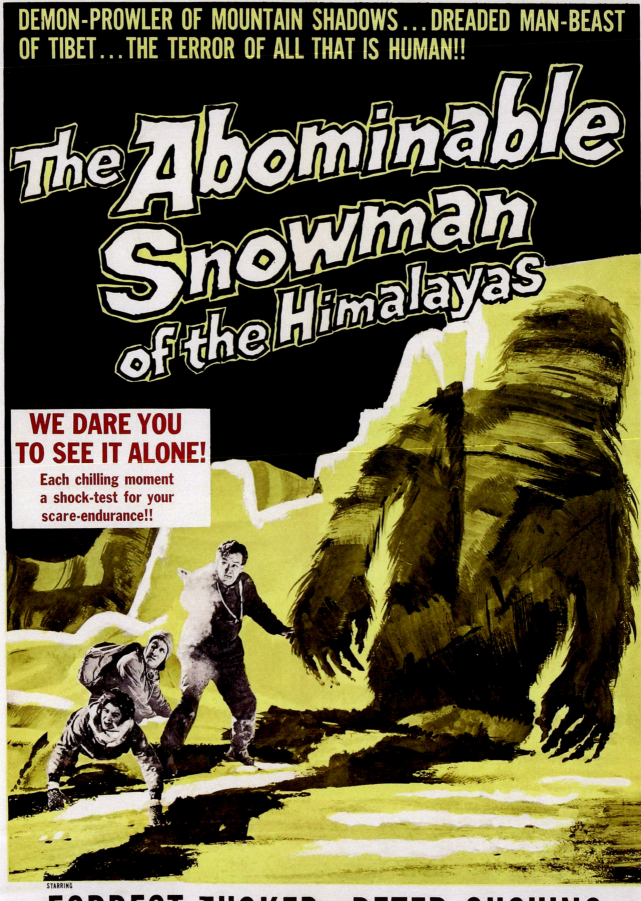

Napier, the Smithsonian scholar, wrote that Bigfoot sightings are easy to dismiss, since so many have been hoaxes. "But if any one of them is real, then as scientists we have a lot to explain," he wrote. "We shall have to admit that there are still major mysteries to be solved in a world we thought we knew so well."

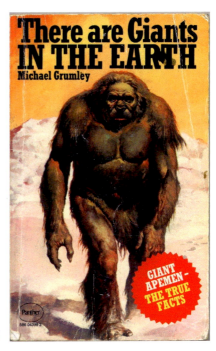

With Bigfoot, as with any unverified fact, people must be careful not to see things that aren't really there: A study published in the *Journal of Zoology* in 2024 noted that Bigfoot sightings were higher in states that had big populations of black bears. But even skeptics such as Darren Naish admit there is still room on Earth for the unknown and possibly unknowable. "I would love to be wrong . . . I still do hope that Bigfoot is real," wrote Naish on his website. "I'm perpetually fascinated by the Bigfoot phenomenon," he says, adding that he's "frankly, shocked and awed by eyewitness accounts, which I really struggle to dismiss," though he cautions that he is not yet convinced.

Still, Naish notes, Bigfoot and other strange phenomena are perhaps most interesting because they are ideas that refuse to fade away, no matter how little evidence there is for them. That raises interesting questions about why humans feel such a deep need to believe in monsters and mysteries. Bigfoot may or may not live in the woods, but it definitely lives in people's hearts—and real or not, perhaps the creature has much to teach humans about themselves.

45

FIELD NOTES

anthropologist—a scientist who studies the history of humankind

authentic—undisputed, based on facts, accurate

bipedal—walking on two feet

cast—a reproduction or impression of an object or image, often made with plaster

cryptid—an animal which some people think might be real but which has never been proven to be real, such as Bigfoot or the Loch Ness Monster

cryptozoology—the study of and search for evidence to prove the existence of legendary or extinct cryptid animals

documentary—a film, television program, or similar work that presents factual subject matter such as history or science

elusive—hard to catch

fossil—the remains or impression of ancient plants or animals preserved in rock

hoax—a humorous or harmful deception; trick

hominid—human or related humanlike creatures, including other primates such as apes, orangutans, and chimpanzees

Neanderthal—a member of the latest-surviving hominid relatives of modern humans known, which lived in Europe and Asia and died out about 30,000 years ago

paleontologist—a scientist who studies ancient animal and plant life

primate—a member of an order of mammals that includes humans, monkeys, apes, and lemurs, among others

skeptical—doubtful

spoor—a footprint, track, or scent of an animal

telepathically—by means of mind-to-mind communication other than the known physical senses

SELECTED BIBLIOGRAPHY

Clark, Jerome. *Encyclopedia of Strange and Unexplained Physical Phenomena*. Detroit, Mich.: Gale Research, 1993.

Lapseritis, Jack "Kewaunee." *The Psychic Sasquatch and Their UFO Connection*. Mill Spring, N.C.: Wild Flower Press, 1998.

Meldrum, Jeff. *Sasquatch: Legend Meets Science*. New York: Forge, 2006.

Napier, John. *Bigfoot: The Yeti and Sasquatch in Myth and Reality*. New York: Dutton, 1973.

Newton, Michael. *Hidden Animals: A Field Guide to Batsquatch, Chupacabra, and Other Elusive Creatures*. Santa Barbara, Calif.: Greenwood Press, 2009.

O'Connor, John. *Secret History of Bigfoot: Field Notes on a North American Monster*. Naperville, Ill.: Sourcebooks, 2024.

Sanderson, Ivan Terence. *Abominable Snowmen: Legend Come to Life: The Story of Sub-Humans on Five Continents from the Early Ice Age until Today*. Philadelphia: Chilton, 1961.

WEBSITES

The Bigfoot Field Researchers Organization
http://www.bfro.net
Explore interactive maps, sighting documentation, research, photos, and sound recordings.

North American Wood Ape Conservancy
https://www.woodape.org
Review this volunteer organization's audio recordings attributed to Bigfoot, database of sightings, and podcast.

Uncovering the Enigma: Sasquatch Sightings
www.pbs.org/video/uncovering-the-enigma-sasquatch-sightings-iaxxnw
Watch a short PBS video about the mystery of Bigfoot.

INDEX

Bigfoot Field Researchers Organization (BFRO), 14, 18, 35, 41
Burns, J. W., 14
Chambers, John, 30
communication, 18
cryptids, 13, 14, 24, 37, 38, 41
cryptozoology, 12, 16, 17, 34
Denisovans, 21
folklore, 13, 29
fossils, 21, 23, 24
Genzoli, Andrew, 17
Gigantopithecus, 24, 41
Gimlin, Bob, 29
Goodall, Jane, 42
habitats
    Canada, 10, 14, 32
    forests, 9, 10, 12, 13, 14, 17, 27, 30, 33, 43, 45
    mountains, 10, 24, 25, 32
    Pacific Northwest, 9, 10, 13, 14, 23
Heuvelmans, Bernard, 16
Hillary, Edmund, 16, 25
Himalayas, 24, 25, 27, 29
hominids, 12, 21, 23
hunting laws, 43
Kaiser, George, 38
Koenigswald, Ralph von, 24
Krantz, Grover, 13, 29, 34, 42
Lapseritis, Jack, 26
Long, Greg, 30
McFeely, Harriett, 35
Meldrum, Jeff, 42
"Minnesota Iceman," 16
Morris, Philip, 30
museums, 32, 35
Naish, Darren, 34, 45
names, 10, 14, 17
Napier, John, 19, 34, 45
Neanderthals, 12, 21, 24, 42
newspapers, 19, 38
Ostman, Albert, 33, 34
Patterson, Roger, 5, 9, 29, 30

physical characteristics
    arms, 9, 27, 29, 30, 37
    colors, 17, 29
    eyes, 18, 27, 37, 38
    feet, 12, 17, 38
    hair, 10, 12, 13, 14, 17, 24, 27, 29, 37, 38, 41
    legs, 30, 33, 37, 41
    odor, 10, 12, 17, 27, 33, 38
    sizes, 17, 24, 27, 33, 37, 38, 42
Roosevelt, Theodore, 30, 33, 37
Sanderson, Ivan, 37
Shipton, Eric, 25
sightings
    at Bluff Creek, 9, 14, 32, 34
    explanations of, 9, 12, 24, 27, 30, 45
    films, 5, 9, 29, 30
    footprints, 10, 13, 14, 17, 25, 27, 30, 32, 34, 37, 38, 40
    and hoaxes, 16, 18, 34, 45
speed, 17–18
Tosh, Kenneth, 38
Van Acker, Christine, 38
Waddell, L. A., 25
Wallace, Ray, 34
Wilson, Helen Smythe, 38
yetis, 14, 15, 16, 24, 25, 27, 29
yowies, 14, 27